20 GREATEST HYMNS

- A Mighty Fortress Is Our God
- All Hail The Power Of Jesus' Name
- Amazing Grace
- Be Thou My Vision
- Blessed Assurance
- Come, Thou Fount of Every Blessing
- Come, Thou Long-Expected Jesus
- He Leadeth Me
- Holy, Holy, Holy
- How Great Thou Art
- It Is Well With My Soul
- Jesus Paid It All
- Jesus Loves Me
- Just As I Am
- Love Divine, All Loves Excelling
- My Hope Is Built On Nothing Less
- O For A Thousand Tongues To Sing
- Rock Of Ages
- To God Be The Glory
- What A Friend We Have In Jesus

ARRANGED BY B. C. DOCKERY

A Mighty Fortress Is Our God

Martin Luther
B. C. Dockery

Arr. ©2022

All Hail the Power of Jesus' Name

Oliver Holden

B. C. Dockery

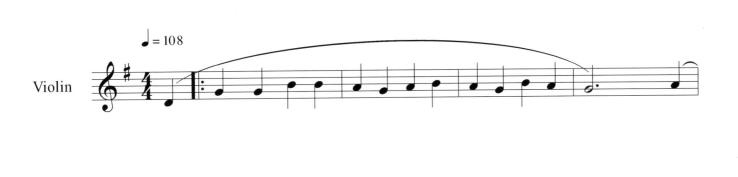

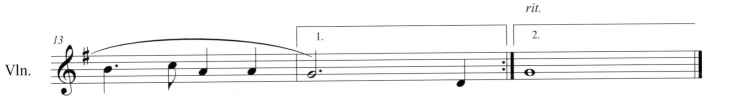

Arr. ©2022

Amazing Grace

John Newton

Be Thou My Vision

Traditional
B. C. Dockery

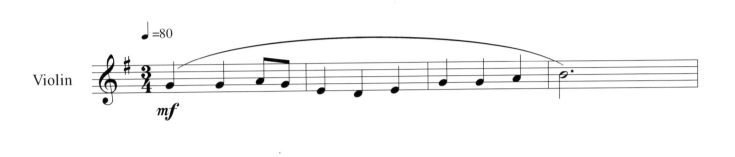

Blessed Assurance

Phoebe P. Knapp

B. C. Dockery

Come, Thou Fount of Every Blessing

Traditional
B. C. Dockery

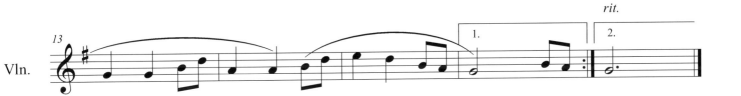

Arr. ©2022

Come, Thou Long-Expected Jesus

Rowland H. Prichard

B. C. Dockery

He Leadeth Me

William B. Bradbury

B. C. Dockery

Arr. ©2022

Holy, Holy, Holy

John, B. Dykes
arr. B. C. Dockery

How Great Thou Art

Traditional
B. C. Dockery

Arr. ©2022

It Is Well with My Soul

Philip P. Bliss
B. C. Dockery

Jesus Paid It All

John T. Grape

Jesus Loves Me

William B. Bradbury

Just as I Am

William B. Bradbury

B. C. Dockery

Arr. ©2022

Love Divine, All Loves Excelling

John Zundel

B. C. Dockery

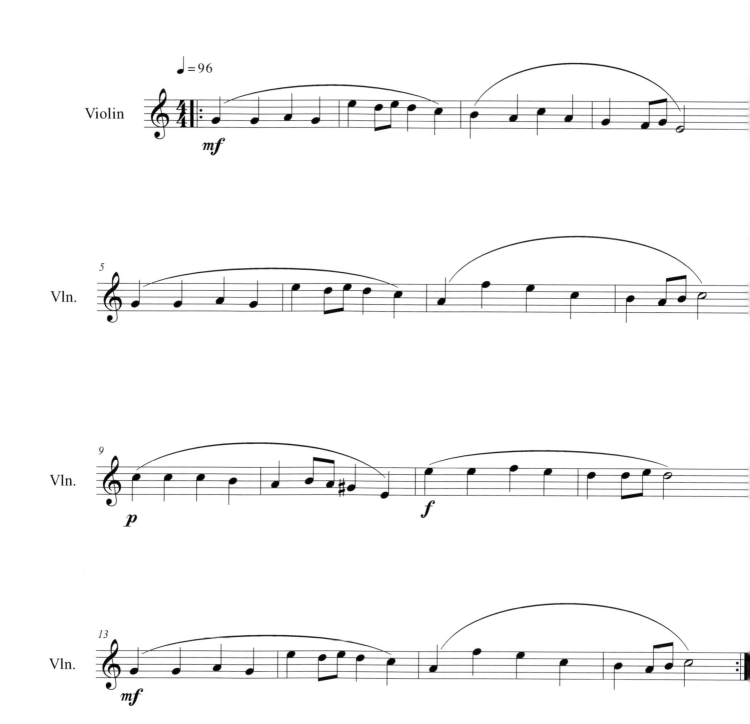

My Hope Is Built On Nothing Less

William B. Bradbury

B. C. Dockery

O for a Thousand Tongues to Sing

Carl G. Glazer

B. C. Dockery

Rock of Ages

Thomas Hastings
B. C. Dockery

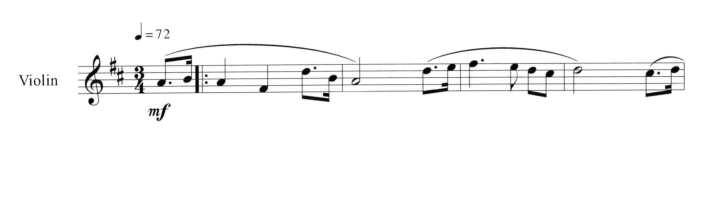

Arr. ©2022

To God Be the Glory

William H. Doane

B. C. Dockery

What a Friend We Have in Jesus

Charles C. Converse

B. C. Dockery

Made in the USA
Monee, IL
27 September 2022

14751150R00015